IMAGES OF ENGLAND

THE WALSALL
LEATHER INDUSTRY

IMAGES OF ENGLAND

THE WALSALL LEATHER INDUSTRY

MICHAEL GLASSON

The
History
Press

Frontispiece: A bridlecutter at D. Mason & Sons in 1953. The making of saddles and bridles have historically been quite separate crafts in Walsall. (Picture courtesy of *Wolverhampton Express and Star*)

First published in 2003 by Tempus Publishing

Reprinted in 2009 by
The History Press
The Mill, Brimscombe Port,
Stroud, Gloucestershire, GL5 2QG
www.thehistorypress.co.uk

Reprinted 2011

British Library Cataloguing in Publication Data.
A catalogue record for this book is available from the British Library.

ISBN 978 0 7524 2793 5

Typesetting and origination by
Tempus Publishing
Printed and bound in England by
Marston Book Services Limited, Oxford.

Contents

Acknowledgements

It is a pleasure to acknowledge the help that I have received in the compilation of this book. My first debt is to all of those Walsall people who, over the past fifteen years, have so kindly lent or donated original photographs to add to the Leather Museum's photographic archive. Starting with just a handful of photographs in 1988, today the collection stands at over 1,200 images. Much of the credit for this is due to my colleague David Mills who has been tireless in tracking down original material to add to the collection. He has also been a great help in the preparation of the current volume. I would also like to thank the following individuals and organisations who have assisted with my research, or who have kindly given permission to reproduce copyright images: Mrs Ann Berwick; Ian Bott; Keith Bryan; *Birmingham Post and Mail*; Alex Carter; Mr A.F. Cooper; Stephen Cox; Mr and Mrs Oliver; Kate Green; John Griffiths; Miss Muriel Hawley; Mrs Joyce Halksworth; Ron Hawkins; Mr Holden-White; Maureen Hunter; Jabez Cliff Ltd; Mr Leon Jessel; Walsall Local History Centre; Mr. Oliver Morton; Pauline Porter; Mr Alan Price; Bill Rollinson; Chris Smart; Mrs Susan Smith; Ruth Vyse; Neil Wadley, *Wolverhampton Express and Star*; *Walsall Observer*; Mr John Ward; Mr J.P. Wilkin; Stuart Williams; Mr Roy Winchester.

Introduction

Early Beginnings

For nearly two hundred years the West Midlands town of Walsall has been the centre of a leather industry that, in the late nineteenth century, grew to be of international significance. Walsall-made saddles, bridles and harness were exported to all corners of the British Empire and beyond, and in the twentieth century they were joined by a host of other leather items: gloves, bags, cases, wallets, dog leads and collars, footballs and belts by the thousand and hundred thousand.

Why Walsall should have developed as such a major leatherworking centre is far from clear. It seems likely, however, that the origins of the trade lie in Walsall's older-established craft of lorinery, or saddler's ironmongery. The loriners were specialist blacksmiths producing a variety of horse-related metalwork such as stirrups, bits, buckles, spurs, and saddle trees (the wood and metal 'skeleton' of a saddle). The essential raw materials for a metalworking industry, including high-grade iron ore, coal and charcoal, could all be found locally. Loriners were working in the town before 1450, and Leland noted on visiting Walsall in around 1540 that there were 'many smiths and bit makers in the town'.

The lorinery trade continued to grow throughout the seventeenth and eighteenth centuries, and by the 1830s it was estimated that local workshops produced sufficient metalwork for 20,000 saddles and 200,000 sets of harness a year. It was around this date that a number of local loriners began to manufacture saddlery and harness. One of the pioneers of the trade was Thomas Newton, a third-generation loriner, who claimed to have produced Walsall's first 'ready-made' riding saddles around the year 1830. The coming of the railways to the area (the Grand Junction in 1837, and the South Staffordshire in 1847) undoubtedly gave a boost to the trade by providing more rapid access to new and existing markets, and a leather quarter soon developed in the streets neighbouring the railway station. The introduction of the sewing machine around 1860

A group of leathergoods preparers at Wincer and Plant in Glebe Street in 1906. Their aprons are immaculate!

gave further impetus to the Walsall trade by helping to speed up production of some items, such as harness traces. By 1861 there were sixty firms making bridles, saddles and harness, together employing over 500 people in the town, plus fifteen tanneries and currying works producing leather.

Walsall, The Horse's Emporium

Horses were vital to everyday life in the Victorian era. Working horses were still the chief means of power on most farms, and they remained essential in the local delivery of goods such as bread, milk and coal. Well-to-do Victorians kept thousands of horses for riding, racing and hunting and for drawing their carriages. It is estimated that in total there were over three million horses in late-Victorian Britain. This vast market for saddlery and harness was supplemented by a flourishing export trade. Surviving ledgers show that Walsall firms exported to most corners of the British Empire, from Antigua to Auckland, as well as to Continental Europe and North and South America.

The steady flow of orders from around the world was boosted by the demands of war. Walsall emerged as a major supplier of military saddlery and harness in the second half of the century, and local manufacturers worked flat out during the Crimean and Franco-Prussian wars, and again during the Boer and First World Wars. Wartime orders could be vast: D. Mason & Sons, for example, produced over 100,000 saddles for the British army during the first two years of the First World War. Even in peacetime there was a continuous demand for various items of military equipment, such as pistol holsters and bandoliers. Mason's stated in 1935 that they had not been without a British Government order at any time in the previous sixty years.

In the last two decades of the nineteenth century, the Walsall leather trade reached its zenith. By 1900 there were over a hundred saddlery and harness companies between them employing nearly 7,000 people, almost a quarter of the national total, and by far the largest concentration of the trade in the UK.

Working Conditions

Despite the apparent prosperity of the late Victorian leather industry, conditions were often very basic for most workers, with long hours and low wages being standard. The Sweated Trades Commission of 1889 investigated the Walsall leather trade and found that conditions were especially bad for women. Even in the most modern factories, women earned half what men did and were expected to stitch leather 2cm (¾in) thick for ten or eleven hours a day, earning perhaps ten shillings a week. Wages of both men and women were further reduced by factory owners deducting money for heating, lighting and 'rent' for the space in which the employee worked. Despite this, trade unionism made little impact on the Walsall leather trade's myriad of small workshops, and conditions were slow to improve. In many workplaces, basic rights such as holiday and sick pay were only introduced well into the twentieth century.

The camaraderie that often developed in leather factories is very evident in this photograph taken at the glove manufacturers Stuart Madeley, c.1975. The friendships made in the workplace frequently lasted a lifetime.

The Rise of Light Leathergoods

The fortunes of Walsall's saddlery and harness trade were intimately linked with the social and economic importance of the horse. With the coming of the motorcar, the traditional roles of the horse were challenged and eventually supplanted, and from 1900 onwards Walsall saddlers and harness makers faced a declining demand for their products. For many years a number of them had been making profitable sidelines such as travelling bags, writing cases, hat boxes, belts, dog leads and collars, and so on. As demand for saddlery and harness dropped away, the more dynamic firms increasingly concentrated on this type of work, and for most of the twentieth century the 'light' or 'fancy' trade was the mainstay of the Walsall leather industry. Some firms specialised in cheap, high-volume items for high-street chains such as Woolworths, while other firms specialised in small runs of luxury items, such as jewellery boxes and handbags in exotic leathers, for exclusive stores in London's Bond Street. After 1920 gloves were also made in the town. By the outbreak of the Second World War there were over seventy firms in Walsall making light leathergoods, probably the greatest concentration in the country outside London.

Harness makers – of all ages and sizes – at D. Mason & Sons, *c*.1930. In contrast to the previous images, this shows an exclusively male environment.

Walsall's saddlery tradition continues: Keith Richardson at Frank Baines Saddlery in Northcote Street checks the seam of a saddle. (Photograph courtesy of Chris Smart)

Recent History

Walsall's leather companies recovered well after the Second World War, responding successfully to the official drive to rebuild export markets. However, from the 1960s they faced increasingly stiff competition from overseas producers, many of them based in developing countries with much lower overheads. Walsall's highly successful gloving industry, for example, was devastated in the 1960s and 1970s by cheap imports from South Korea and Japan. By the end of the twentieth century intense competition from overseas producers, especially in south-east Asia, had resulted in the closure of many of Walsall's leathergoods factories.

The cheap high-volume end of the market is today almost entirely met by imports: China alone exported leather items to the value of 12 billion dollars in 2002. The remaining leathergoods industry in Walsall specialises in the highest quality goods, destined for luxury markets in the United States, Japan and Continental Europe as well as London's West End. Walsall factories produce leathergoods for some of the world's most famous brands, and include a number of Royal Warrant Holders including Launer for handbags and small leathergoods, G. Ettinger for leathergoods and Jabez Cliff for saddlery and lorinery.

One of the most positive developments in recent years has been the recovery of Walsall's saddlery trade. The growing popularity of horse riding from the 1960s onwards brought with it increased demand for saddlery, bridles and other horse tack, and what had been a dying industry was dramatically revived. The post-war period saw a number of innovations, one of the most important developments being the introduction of the laminated 'multibond' plywood saddle tree, patented by Walsall man Len Holmes, and now in almost universal use. Walsall saddles have the reputation of being among the best in the world and there is currently a flourishing export trade. At the beginning of the twenty-first century there are approximately seventy Walsall-based firms making saddlery and bridles.

Throughout its long and complicated history, the Walsall leather industry has demonstrated the tenacity and resourcefulness of local people. Faced with constant challenges from the outside world, Walsall's leatherworkers have responded with flexibility and ingenuity. At the beginning of the twenty-first century the leather industry is a rare example of a traditional craft-based trade that, despite its apparently unchanging nature, has successfully managed to adapt and respond to meet new demands and new opportunities. With such a tradition behind it, there are good reasons to be optimistic about the future of the industry!

one

Tanning and
Currying

Tanning is one of Walsall's oldest leather industries, having been established here by the mid-fifteenth century. In the seventeenth century there were at least two tanneries in existence, in Lower Rushall Street and Digbeth, both presumably drawing water from the Walsall Brook, a tributary of the River Tame. However, they seem to have been operating on a small scale. It has often been said that Walsall became a centre of the saddlery trade because of its tanneries, but there is little evidence to support this. At the period the saddlery trade was taking off in Walsall, in the 1830s and 1840s, the town possessed just one working tannery employing about five people, and it is clear that much of the leather used by Walsall's leatherworkers was being tanned elsewhere.

As the saddlery and harness trades expanded, the rising demand for leather encouraged the growth of a currying trade in the town. Currying is the process of impregnating the tanned leather with fats and oils, to render it flexible, hardwearing and water resistant, and of finishing it to produce an attractive appearance. By the late nineteenth century Walsall had a thriving currying industry, which successfully adapted to producing light leathers for small leathergoods after 1900.

Walsall's five-hundred-year history as a tanning town ended in 1970 when the last of its tanneries relocated to Scotland. A combination of cheap foreign imports, from low-wage economies, increasingly strict regulations on water quality and the disposal of industrial waste, and their relatively small size, made Walsall's tanneries uncompetitive. Happily there are still two curriers operating in the town, producing a range of specialist leathers for the saddlery and leathergoods markets.

The workforce of Messrs Handford Greatrex & Brother in 1888. The tannery covered a large area between Lichfield Street and Lower Rushall Street, today the site of Safeway's supermarket. The firm was described in 1889 as a producer of coach, saddle, bridle, and harness leather, and japanned and enamelled horsehides for the shoe trade. The two Greatrex brothers, partners in the business, are thought to be standing on the extreme left and right of this photograph.

Albert and Evangeline Greatrex and their children outside Moss Close, their ornate Gothic house in Mellish Road in 1890. Albert's cousin, Arthur Whitehouse Greatrex , seen in the previous photograph, had moved here by 1901. Moss Close eventually passed into institutional use and was demolished in the 1960s.

Members of the Greatrex family at Spring Hill, Jesson Road, c.1905. Arthur Whitehouse Greatrex is seated on the steps. Spring Hill was the home of his wife's brother, Thomas Hill. As well as being a rare record of a now vanished house, this is thought to be one of the earliest photographs of a motorcar in Walsall.

The Manufacture of Leather.

1. Hide, showing commercial divisions: *cc*, cheeks; *sh*, shoulder; *ss*, shanks; *b*, belly; *bt*, butt.
2. Puering and bating vats. 3. Unhairing. 4. Knives for unhairing and fleshing. 5. Interior of tannery. 6. Currying shop. 7. Shaving a skin of parchment. 8. Stuffing-drum. 9. Rubbing down skins after dyeing. 10. Coating and drying 'patent' leather.

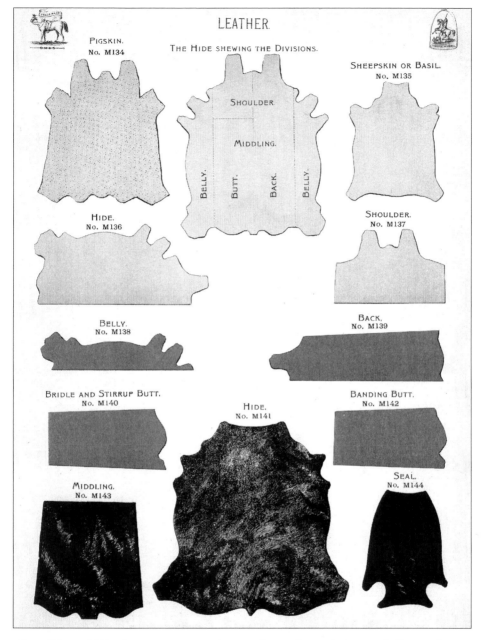

LEATHER.

THE HIDE SHEWING THE DIVISIONS.

PIGSKIN.
No. M134

SHOULDER.

MIDDLING.

BELLY. BUTT. BACK. BELLY.

SHEEPSKIN OR BASIL.
No. M135

HIDE.
No. M136

SHOULDER.
No. M137

BELLY.
No. M138

BACK.
No. M139

BRIDLE AND STIRRUP BUTT.
No. M140

HIDE.
No. M141

BANDING BUTT.
No. M142

MIDDLING.
No. M143

SEAL.
No. M144

Above: Skins and hides from a D. Mason & Sons catalogue of around 1900. Walsall's speciality was the production of heavy cow hides and pigskins for the saddlery trade, the latter used for saddle seats and small leathergoods such as coin purses.

Opposite: 'The Manufacture of Leather', from an encyclopedia of around 1905. Tanning was a messy and smelly business. Puering (No.2 on the illustration) is the process of treating the skins with a warm infusion of dog excrement, which, through the action of enzymes, helps to remove any remaining lime, and produce a soft and stretchy leather. Bating achieves the same result using pigeon or hen droppings.

Left: 'Unhairing Skins', an illustration from a children's book, *c.*1920. Having been immersed in a solution of lime, the skins are ready for unhairing. This was achieved by placing the skin over a wooden beam, and scraping it with a two-handled curved knife. Following this process, the skins would then have any remaining flesh removed.

Below: The workforce of the Leamore Currying Co., Providence Lane, in 1919. This was one of thirty-five currying concerns in the town at this date. The growth of the light leathergoods trade after 1900 gave a boost to the local currying trade by creating a demand for a wide range of printed and coloured leathers.

The rough leather store at D. Mason & Sons in Marsh Lane, c.1930. Although primarily leathergoods manufacturers, Masons also operated their own currying works at the rear of their Marsh Street site, buying rough tanned leather from elsewhere and supplying finished leather to the trade.

D. Mason & Sons currying workshop in Marsh Lane, c.1930. This building still survives and is partially occupied by a saddlery firm today. The windows on the upper floor are designed to swivel to catch the breeze and assist with the drying process.

Scouring leather at D. Mason & Sons. The scouring process involves cleaning up the grain surface of the leather after tanning, using slate scrapers or slickers.

Shaving or 'flatting' leather by hand at D. Mason & Sons, c.1930. A highly skilled process, the leather was placed over a beam or 'peg' and shaved to the required thickness using a two-handled knife. Machines had existed since the mid-nineteenth century to do this, but for the best quality leather hand shaving was specified, since it was thought to disturb the fibres of the leather less. Hand shaving was still being practised in the 1960s.

Hand staining case hides at D. Mason & Sons, c.1930. Dye is being gently brushed onto the hides. Buckets of dye can be seen in the foreground. The experienced colour mixer who knew the correct formula for each required colour had almost sacred status in many tanneries and guarded his recipes jealously.

A group of workmen from E.T. Holden & Son, c.1930. These men worked in the spray shop, where they would have sprayed the tanned leather with dyestuffs. This was a quicker process than hand staining, but less satisfactory for heavy-duty leathers, since the dye penetrated less deeply. The men include Frank Grey on the right, and possibly Alan Owen second from the left.

Left: Straining upholstery hides at Handford Greatrex, *c.*1935. The partially tanned hides are being stretched in a damp state. As well as helping to reduce the wrinkles or growth marks in the leather, this process also helped to increase the surface area of the hide, meaning extra profit for the tanner since hides were always sold by area. The hides in this photograph were destined for Rolls Royce Motors.

Below: One of the largest tanning and currying businesses in Walsall was that of E.T. Holden & Sons. E.T. Holden inherited the firm at the age of nineteen and built up its reputation for pigskins and japanned or patent leather. He was three times mayor of the town and became its MP in 1891. Four generations of the Holden family are shown in this image from around 1922, from left to right: Sir E.T. Holden, his daughter Mrs Holden-White, her son Lt.-Cdr Thomas White, and his newly born son Thomas Holden-White, who eventually became managing director of the company.

Above: A recently discovered postcard showing the aftermath of a major fire at E.T. Holden's tannery in Park Street, *c.*1910. The fire gutted the currying building, but the sheds in the foreground, which covered the tanning pits, appear to be untouched. Fires were a constant hazard at tanneries and currying works since over time the buildings became saturated with flammable oils and fats, which meant that any fire would take hold very rapidly.

Overleaf above: The Queen's Coronation being celebrated at E.T. Holden in 1953. Each employee was presented with a bottle of wine and a chicken to mark the occasion.

Overleaf below: A new thirty-foot long boiler being delivered to the E.T. Holden tannery in Park Street in the 1950s. Access to the site was very constricted, consisting of a narrow passageway at the side of the New Inns, and chaos seems to be resulting! Note the trolley bus in what is now Walsall's busiest pedestrianised street.

The E.T. Holden workforce enjoying the annual works outing to Llangollen in 1953. The works outing or 'gypsy party' was something of an institution in most large Walsall workplaces at this date. Ron Hawkins who attended this outing recalls that senior staff and those of a more delicate constitution were able to return on an earlier coach, while those left behind indulged in some serious revelling at the firm's expense.

The visit of the Leather Retailers Association to E.T. Holden Ltd in October 1959. Alan Owen, with the spray gun, is demonstrating how pigskins are dyed. Alan Hodson, the manager, is on the right of the picture, with assistant manager Ron Hawkins beside him. E.T. Holden was renowned for the quality of its pigskins and in the 1960s was a regular supplier to the Italian leathergoods company Gucci. The firm relocated to the Scottish Borders in 1970 and the site was redeveloped for the Saddlers Centre shopping arcade. (Photograph courtesy of *Walsall Observer*)

Mr Miles splitting leather at Edward Price & Son, 1969. (Photograph courtesy of Alan Price)

Above left: An unidentified currier at D. Mason & Sons in 1953. He is applying oil to heavy hides with a cloth 'wad' as part of the currying process. The key to currying is impregnating the leather with oils and greases, to ensure that the lubricated fibres move easily against each other, thereby helping to increase the leather's flexibility and suppleness, as well as its water resistance. (Photograph courtesy of *Wolverhampton Express and Star*)

Above right: Gilbert Greatrex of the tanning firm Handford Greatrex & Co. Handford Greatrex occupied one of the oldest tannery sites in the town, which had been in operation since at least the seventeenth century. In its later years a major supplier of leather to Clark's Shoes, the company was taken over by Harvey's of Nantwich in 1961, and closed three years later.

Left: Doris Devey and a colleague 'toggling' leather on a frame at Edward Price Ltd in 1969. Toggling helps to keep the leather taut while drying, preventing creases reappearing in the leather.

Left: Leather being measured on a Murphy measuring machine at the curriers Edward Price Ltd in South Street in 1969. These machines used a series of pins to measure the exact area of hide or skin. When confronted by a similar machine at Connolly's currying works in London, the great illustrator W. Heath Robinson admitted that he could not have invented a more bizarre-looking machine himself.

Below left: This photograph is thought to show the process of 'drenching' hides in a bran solution at Edward Price Ltd in 1969. The fermenting bran produces a mild acid that neutralises any lime remaining from the liming process, and helps to open the pores of the skins or hides, ready for tanning.

Below right: Machine setting at Edward Price Ltd in 1969. 'Setting out' is the process of removing the wrinkles or growth marks in the leather. It is normally done by hand using a slicker but the machine shown in this photograph (referred to by some curriers as the 'motorbike') helps to take some of the physical effort out of the task.

Right: Bill Walker, currier, at Edward Price Ltd. This and the following two photographs were taken as part of a study of the leather trade by photographer Chris Smart, commissioned by the Leather Museum in 1998.

Below: Barry Smith stoning leather at Edward Price Ltd in 1998. The process of stoning is another method of giving a smooth surface to the leather.

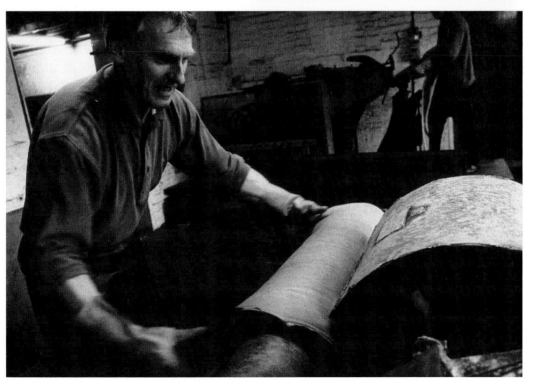

Keith Ford rounding leather at Edward Price Ltd in 1998. Rounding is the process of cutting away any leather around the edges of the hide that may have been marked by the toggling process.

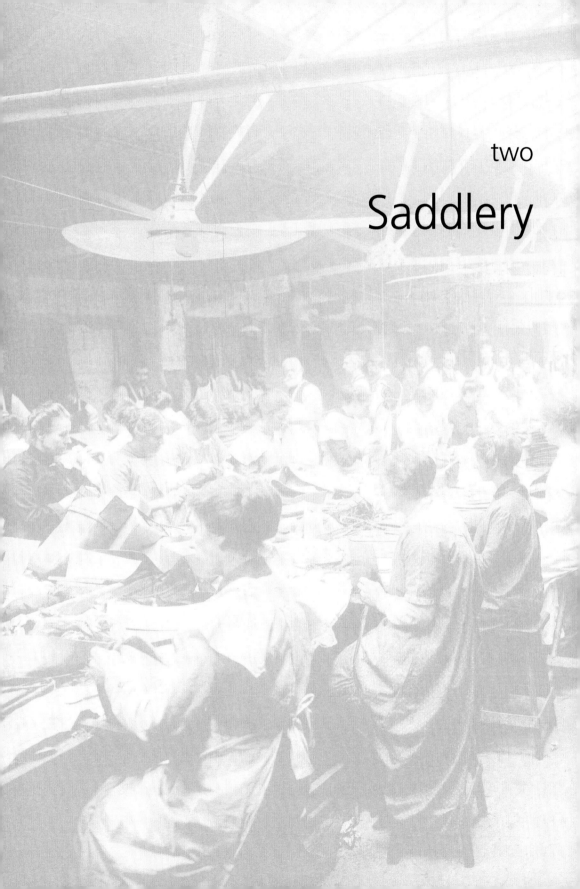

two

Saddlery

Over the past two centuries Walsall has been home to a remarkable variety of leatherworking trades, but there is no question that it is saddlery which has been the most enduring of these and for which the town remains most famous. Not surprisingly, there are many reminders of the trade around the town: the little known 'angel' saddler carved on the front of the Council House, the Saddlers Centre shopping mall in the town centre (itself partly built on the site of a tannery), and the nickname of the town's football team, the Saddlers, to name but three examples.

The golden age of Walsall's saddlery trade was the late nineteenth century, when Britain's horse population probably exceeded three million. With the coming of the motorcar, the use of horses went into decline, and for much of the twentieth century saddle-making was seen as a dying trade, serving an ever-smaller market, with an ageing workforce.

The growth in riding for pleasure since the 1960s brought about a dramatic revival in the fortunes of the Walsall saddlery trade. The number of saddlery companies multiplied as young saddlers completed their apprenticeships and set up on their own. Today there are over seventy firms making a huge variety of saddles for export to most parts of the world, and a large number of allied manufacturers producing riding clothing, horse brushes, saddle trees, whips, and bits and stirrups, and so on. The town's reputation for high-quality saddles and bridles is being actively promoted, and Walsall can once again proudly claim to be the world centre of the saddlery trade.

Thomas Newton claimed to be the first Walsall manufacturer to produce 'ready- made' saddles, around the year 1830. Like many of the pioneers of the Walsall saddlery trade, he was a loriner or saddler's ironmonger by background, inheriting the family business at the age of eighteen.

Thomas Newton's business was a success (despite his brother, who acted as his agent in California, killing himself in an explosion on the goldfields) and within a few years he was exporting saddlery and harness worldwide. He claimed to have been the first local saddler to export goods to Australia. Newton's catalogue of saddlery and harness, published *c*.1870, is one of the finest ever produced. Newton drew most of the illustrations himself, and was clearly a talented artist.

A particularly fine engraving from Newton's *Saddlery of All Nations*. A few years later Eadweard Muybridge would publish photographs that radically altered opinions about the action of horses in motion.

Above: The saddle-tree-making workshop of Thomas Lote Woollatt at 41 Birmingham Street, *c.*1900, close to the present day site of the Blue Coat Comprehensive School. The saddle tree is the wood and metal 'skeleton' of the saddle. The men in this scene are using drawshaves to shape the trees, which were normally made from beech wood. The men wear a harness over their shoulders, which carries a block on their chest, designed to support the tree as they work on it.

Left: The superb frontispiece of William Overton and Co.'s 1903 catalogue of saddlery and harness. The company's factory and its neighbour, belonging to John Leckie & Co., dominated the east side of Goodall Street, making it one of the gloomier streets in the town.

Right: The more modest factory of E.J. Parkes in Holtshill Lane, illustrated in a catalogue of 1902, was much more typical of the trade. It was one of a number of factories erected around the time of the Boer War, a boom time for most Walsall saddlery manufacturers. The building is now the Walsall factory of Launer, Royal Warrant Holders for handbags and small leathergoods to HM The Queen.

Below: Military contracts were of great importance to the Walsall leather trade. This illustration comes from *The Four-in-Hand*, a catalogue produced in 1905 by R.E. Thacker, saddlers and ironmongers of Green Lane.

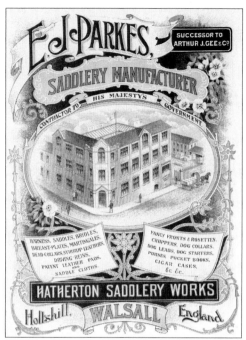

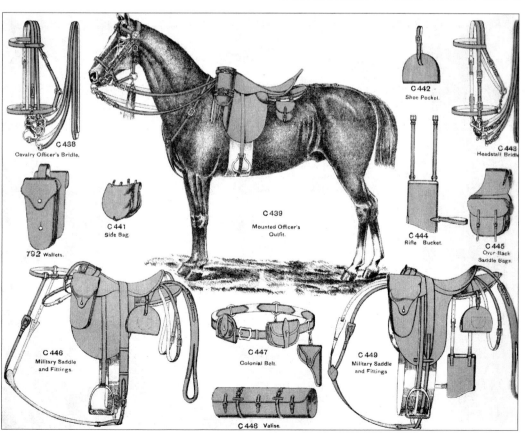

C 438
Cavalry Officer's Bridle.

C 442
Shoe Pocket.

C 443
Headstall Bridle

C 441
Side Bag

C 439
Mounted Officer's
Outfit.

C 444
Rifle Bucket.

C 445
Over-Back
Saddle Bags

792 Wallets.

C 446
Military Saddle
and Fittings.

C 447
Colonial Belt.

C 449
Military Saddle
and Fittings

C 448 Valise.

Horses would have been a familiar sight on the streets of Victorian and Edwardian Walsall. Here we see the delivery van of G. Attkins & Son of 5 Park Street, grocers and wine and spirit merchants.

A fine photograph of a working horse, *c.*1900, taken in Burton-on-Trent. Walsall harness makers and loriners were capable of producing every item worn by this horse, including the buckles and chains, the cart saddle, the collar with its projecting metal hames, the plume on the horse's head, and even its shoes!

The horse and cart of Pelari's, Walsall's celebrated ice-cream makers. The driver is Mr Bassett, and his four-year-old passenger is George Yates. (Photograph courtesy of Mrs Ann Berwick)

The demand for harness for farm horses remained substantial up until the time of the Second World War, when large numbers of imported tractors were used on British farms for the first time. In this view horses are bringing in the hay harvest 'at Barr', presumably somewhere near Great Barr.

Above: The horse and cart of Tommy Hartshorne, Walsall coal merchant, splendidly decorated for a May Day parade, *c.*1930. Like many of Walsall's coal merchants, Hartshorne was based close to the canal, in Short Street.

Left: Joseph Leckie, seen here in 1917. His father John was a Glasgow saddler who established a Walsall branch of the business in 1874. The firm specialised in military contracts, supplying huge quantities of saddlery and harness to the British Army. Joseph served as the town's MP between 1931 and 1938 and earned a special place in the affections of local people as one of Walsall's greatest philanthropists.

Previous pages: Producing pack saddles at D. Mason & Sons, *c.*1910. Rows of women are busy stitching leather components together, tedious and physically tiring work. Daniel Mason's son Rowland was summoned to give evidence to a House of Lord's Select Commission on the sweated trades in 1889, and was closely questioned about the nature of this work.

Above: The John Leckie & Co. workforce on a factory outing to Matlock in 1912. At its peak around 1900 the company had 300 employees, and would hire its own excursion train.

Right: The John Leckie & Co. stand at the British Industries Fair in 1920. Following the First World War, a great deal of army surplus saddlery was sold off cheaply, which depressed the market for several years. Leckie & Co. fortunately made a wide variety of other leather items such as belts, footballs, and cases, which helped the firm to survive. It eventually merged with D. Mason & Sons in 1928.

At Mason's Marsh Street factory, *c.*1930, and little has changed in saddle-making since Victorian times. It remains a highly skilled craft with little evidence of any mechanisation. Piles of completed saddles await collection.

Stitchers at Heath Machin, Teddesley Street, Walsall, *c.*1890. Heath Machin specialised in the making of reins at this date; they later became manufacturers of dog leads and collars, and light leathergoods. The woman on the right may well be the firm's owner, Elizabeth Heath.

Above: A recently discovered photograph showing women stitchers from Messrs E. Jeffries & Son, bridle manufacturers of Mountrath Street, *c.*1902. The sixteen-year-old Emily Booker is kneeling on the right. The stitching of leather was generally considered to be women's work in Walsall. Male bridlemakers were always referred to as bridlecutters in the town, emphasising that they did not stitch.

Right: The sewing machine made limited headway in the Walsall saddlery and harness trade. Although sewing machines were being used as early as 1860 by at least one local manufacturer, hand-sewn saddlery and harness was considered safer, and as a result commanded a better price. This was presumably because hand stitching was less likely to 'run' if a thread snapped.

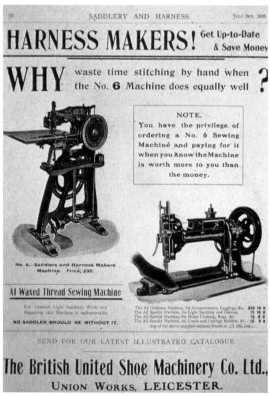

43

The Machine Sewing Department at Hampson & Scott, Whittimere Street, probably in the 1890s. Even in the largest and most modern saddlery and harness factories, hand stitching remained the norm, and machine stitching was limited to certain items such as harness traces.

Hand stitching harness straps at D. Mason & Sons, Marsh Street in 1953. The leather is held tightly in the jaws of the 'clam', and stitched with two needles, one attached to each end of the thread. The thread is pulled tight at each stitch to ensure that it is locked in place and cannot run should the thread break. The woman in the foreground is thought to be Mrs Agnes Dyde. She is wearing a leather 'ockle' to protect her finger. Leonard Mason noted in 1950 'very few hand-stitchers are entering industry. The work is very hard and tedious'. (Photograph courtesy of *Walsall Observer*)

The making of horse collars is a highly specialised branch of the harness trade, taking many years to learn. In this view of Augustus Stubbs' workshop in Lime Street, *c.*1905, the workmen are sitting cross-legged on boxes. They are using long metal stuffing irons to pack straw tightly inside the collar. Collarmakers' mallets, the head normally made of lignum vitae, can be seen lying on the ground.

The yard at Augustus Stubbs' workshop. A selection of the company's collars hang on the workshop wall. One of the men holds a stuffing iron, and more mallets can be seen in the foreground. This workshop is today the home of Keith Bryan Saddlery, and has been in continuous use for saddle and harness–making for well over a century.

Left: A postcard sent in 1910 from Western Australia, to Brace, Windle, Blyth & Co., Walsall leathergoods manufacturers. A handwritten inscription on the reverse states 'we are well satisfied with the collarmaker which you sent out being a first class workman'. The workman's name is recorded as 'Heydon', but the name of the aboriginal man in the photograph is not recorded.

Below: Harriet Collington at E. Hawley & Co. in Hill Street in 1948. Harriet began working for the company in 1878 and stayed with E. Hawley for seventy years, continuing to make slipper stirrups for sidesaddles long after the factory had moved into primarily making light leathergoods. Her seventieth anniversary was celebrated at the factory with the custom of 'knocking out' – beating the benches with hammers to make as much noise as possible.

Above: American GIs watch an elderly saddler 'setting' a saddle seat at Frank Ringrose Ltd in Midland Road during Anglo-American Friendship Week in 1945. A pile of wool flock, used to stuff the seat, is ready on the bench.

Right: Eric Davies in the warehouse at D. Mason & Sons, Marsh Street in 1953. Horse collars hang from a beam, and a batch of mule collars with their distinctive scallop-shaped blinkers can be seen in the foreground. These would have been destined for export. (Picture courtesy of *Wolverhampton Express and Star*)

Frank Mumford of Jabez Cliff in 1963. A superb craftsman, it was said that his saddles were so good that they were never checked, only counted. He began his working life during the Boer War, at the age of thirteen, starting by staining and polishing the edges of cut leather. He finally retired in 1964, after more than sixty years' work in the trade. (Photograph courtesy of *Wolverhampton Express and Star*)

By 1970, when this photograph was taken, Walsall's great saddlery revival was well under way, and youngsters were once again being recruited. The Green Lane Saddle Co. employees seen here include Dave Connors, nearest to the camera, and Phil Brown (with beard).

Mel Beck at Walsall Riding Saddle Ltd, Garden Street, in 1998. The company was founded by Len Holmes, who patented the use of laminated ply saddle trees, one of the major developments in saddle-making in the twentieth century. (Photograph courtesy of Chris Smart)

Nellie York applying stain to the edges of a leather saddle component, at Walsall Riding Saddle in 1998. It is important that the edges are smooth so as not to cut the horse, and that they match the colour of the rest of the saddle. (Photograph courtesy of Chris Smart)

Above: Barry Broadhurst at Frank Baines Saddlery, using a staple gun to attach webs to the saddle tree in 1998. There have been relatively few significant changes in saddlery production in the twentieth century. The use of laminated ply saddle trees, staple guns, and increased use of sewing machines for much of the stitching are probably the major developments. (Photograph courtesy of Chris Smart)

Left: Alex Carter at Keith Bryan Saddlery in Lime Street, 1990. Alex is thought to be the only woman saddler currently working in Walsall. She is a past winner in the 'Saddler of the Year' awards organised by the Society of Master Saddlers. The factory in which she is working is the former Augustus Stubbs horse-collar workshop, seen in the photograph on p.45. (Photograph courtesy of Kate Green)

three

Light
Leathergoods

The making of light or fancy leathergoods became an increasingly important part of the Walsall leather trades after 1900, as demand for saddlery and harness began to decline. The term 'light leathergoods' was used for purses, wallets, bags, watch straps, jewel boxes, desk equipment such as blotters, and a host of personal accessories such as cigar cases and manicure sets. However, in most factories it excluded cases and travel goods, which would generally be made in another workshop.

By 1931 the light leathergoods trade in Walsall was employing more people than the saddlery and harness trade, and this remained true until saddle-making recovered in the late twentieth century. The new trade employed large numbers of women, and in most factories women outnumbered men by at least four to one, something that is reflected in many of the following photographs.

Opposite above: Leathergoods preparers at Wincer & Plant in 1906. Preparing workshops were generally well lit, as the work was often of an intricate nature. 'Marbles' can be seen on the bench. These were usually old lithographic printing stones, which were valued because they provided a firm smooth surface for working on. Each preparer would be allocated his or her own marble.

Leathercutters at Wincer & Plant Ltd, Glebe Street, in 1906. Leathercutters were the elite of the leathergoods trade, earning the highest wages. They would aim to maximise the potential of a skin or hide with the minimum of waste, taking into account any scars and holes in the leather, and its natural grain and pattern. Cutting benches can be seen on the left, with leather-covered strops for sharpening the cutting or clicking knives.

Sewing machinists at Wincer & Plant in 1906. Sewing machines were in use in the Walsall leather industry by 1860, but they made little impact until the leathergoods trade developed after 1900. These splendid Singer sewing machines appear to be powered by electricity, which was available in Walsall from 1895.

This photograph is thought to show Mr Plant of Wincer & Plant with his office staff in 1906. It is one of a series of photographs in the museum's collection, which for many years were unidentified, but are now known to have been taken at this factory. Mr Plant was said to be 'very particular' about the way his employees dressed, something that can be seen in the previous photographs.

The employees of James Homer Ltd in the late 1920s. The company's address is listed as 'back of No.78 Mill Lane', indicating that like so many Walsall leather factories and workshops it had been built on cheaper land at the rear of a row of houses or shops. The company is still operating from these premises today, and is now part of G. Ettinger Ltd, leathergoods manufacturers by appointment to HRH the Prince of Wales.

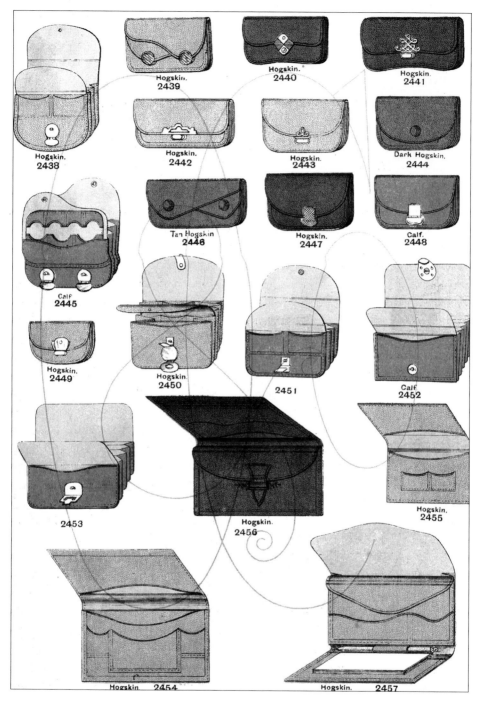

Typical light leathergoods from the Walsall manufacturer Overton & Co.'s catalogue of around 1900.

Above: The workforce of John More & Co., Wolverhampton Street, *c.*1927. Originally saddlery and harness manufacturers, by the 1920s the company was making a range of leathergoods.

Left: Frank Cooper with a new stitching machine (referred to by the workforce as the 'cracker') at John More & Co. Mr Cooper worked for the firm for fifty-three years. His wife was working as a machinist at the factory when he first met her.

Opposite above: Originating as a saddlery and harness manufacturer, by 1930 D. Mason & Sons was one of the town's biggest leathergoods makers. Here a predominantly female workforce is preparing light leathergoods at the firm's Marsh Street factory.

Opposite below: Making school satchels at D. Mason & Sons, *c.*1930. The man in the foreground is cutting leather by hand. Sewing machinists can be seen behind him, bent over their machines.

The trade stand of Messrs Broadhurst & Thompson at the British Industries Fair in Birmingham, c.1930. The firm was one of three in the town at this date specialising in the manufacture of bag and purse frames. The large number of suppliers in the town must have given Walsall's leathergoods manufacturers substantial competitive advantage over rival firms based in smaller centres of the trade.

A 'dorothy' or drawstring bag made by Patterson & Stone of Frederick Street, in a style very popular in the 1920s and '30s.

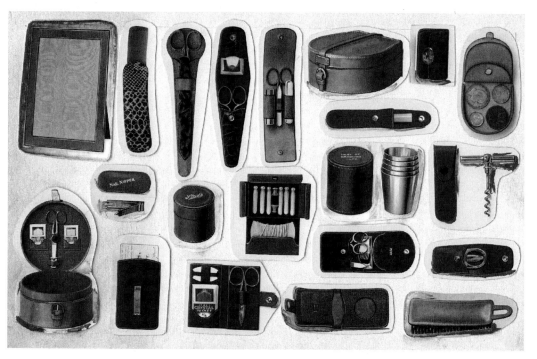

Novelty leathergoods from a Patterson & Stone catalogue paste-up of about 1930, including manicure sets, sewing sets, boxes for detachable shirt collars, and a leather-covered picture frame. These are the kind of items that were made in huge quantities for the high street stores of the day. A single order from a large retailer such as Woolworths might run to 30,000 of a particular item. Such large orders could become very tedious for the workforce!

Handbags designed by Frank Jennings in 1938. Frank was a talented designer who worked for J. Jones, manufacturers of high-quality leathergoods, before setting up his own company. A photograph of one of his designs was featured in *Art and Industry*, Herbert Read's classic work on industrial design. Frank lived in Lumley Road in Chuckery for many years.

Above: The workforce of E. Hawley & Co, leathergoods manufacturers, enjoying a social gathering at the Rendezvous Café near the entrance to the Arboretum, *c.*1938. The occasion was the twenty-first birthday of one of the Hawley family. Herbert Hawley, the owner of the company, is seated in the centre of the photograph.

Opposite above: Whitehouse Cox was established in the mid-nineteenth century making saddler's ironmongery. Later the firm became manufacturers of saddlery, dog equipment, light leathergoods and gloves. This photograph, dating from 1935, shows the warehouse and despatch department at the company's factory in Marsh Street. Malcolm Cox is on the left of the photograph.

Opposite below: Mrs Amanda Cox of Whitehouse Cox in 1935. Mrs Cox was probably the most senior woman in the Walsall leather trade at this date, and during the Second World War she ran the company as managing director, while her sons were on military service. A picture of the company's impressive Marsh Street factory, erected in 1890, hangs on the wall.

During the Second World War most Walsall leather factories concentrated on producing equipment for the war effort. Materials for leathergoods production were hard to come by unless they contributed directly to this end. Patterson & Stone, for example, made leather flying helmets for the RAF. Here six of their employees take a break from work. Kathleen Hunt is wearing the helmet.

An excellent view of a sadly as-yet-unidentified leathergoods factory thought to be in the Springhill Road area of Walsall in 1948. The workforce is making jewellery boxes. After the war there was an official drive to build up export markets, and thereby earn foreign currency to help rebuild the country. However, manufacturers were hampered by punitive levels of purchase tax, which made their products very expensive for the home market.

A Christmas party at Patterson & Stone in 1950. Music was provided by the accordionist in the foreground, and generous sprigs of mistletoe decorate the workshop. This photograph gives some impression of the extent to which women outnumbered men in the light leathergoods industry by this date.

The press room at E. Hawley & Co. in 1953. Machine cutting of leather using hydraulic presses increasingly replaced hand cutting in the twentieth century: it was a quick and efficient method where a large number of a particular item was being produced. For smaller runs of items it was probably not cost effective to have press knives made. Tom Jinks is seen here in the middle of the photograph.

Leathergoods preparers hard at work at E. Hawley & Co. in Hill Street, *c*.1950. Note the two teapots in the foreground! Tea-making was often assigned to the youngest recruit to the workforce. The four women on the right are, from left to right: Nellie Phillips, Mrs Philpott, Pat Gadsby, Mrs Perks.

An unidentified leathergoods preparer at D. Mason & Sons in 1953. She is gluing a zip into a letter case ready for stitching. The glue was traditionally made from rendered-down animal hooves, and had to be heated before it could be used. Like tea-making, this was often a job given to the youngest employee. Today artificial adhesives are generally used. The preparer's marble, a litho-graphic printing stone, can clearly be seen. (Photograph courtesy of *Wolverhampton Express and Star*)

Above: Clare Atkinson, bottom right, 'machining' school satchels at D. Mason & Sons in 1953. Racks of press knives can be seen hanging on the wall These would be used to cut out leather components on a press. (Photo-graph courtesy of *Walsall Observer*)

Left: A group of John More & Co. handbag preparers and framers and their friends enjoying a week's holiday at Blackpool in the late 1950s. Paid holidays were becoming more usual for leatherworkers by this date. Strong and long-lasting friendships were often made at work. Front row, left to right: Jessie Evans, Hazel ?, Sheila ?, Lily Guest. Back row: Joyce Halksworth (daughter of Jessie Evans), Doreen ?, Maureen Barrett, Barbara ?, and Maureen Hunter.

'A dash to row on the lake, John More's dinner time.' Brenda Withey and Doreen Baker rowing on the Arboretum lake in the late 1950s.

A group of staff from John More & Co. on an outing, c.1948. (Photograph courtesy of Mr A.F. Cooper)

Above: The workforce of Messrs Yates Brothers at their Whitehouse Street factory in 1967. This is presumably the preparing shop as marbles and gluepots (each with its own gas jet to keep the glue warm) are much in evidence. Shoe-cleaning kits are being assembled in the foreground.

Right: An unidentified woman goldblocking leathergoods at Leon Jessel Ltd in Corporation Street, *c.*1978. Goldblocking involves pressing a heated embossed die onto a strip of metallic foil to 'block' a permanent inscription or motif onto the leather. Established by Leon Jessel, a Jewish refugee from Germany, this company specialised in making high-quality leathergoods for leading stores such as Harrods.

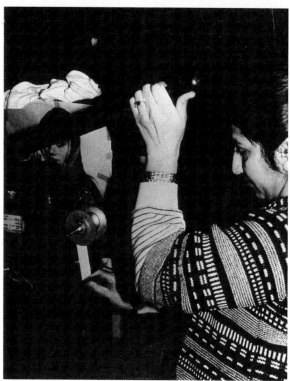

Mr Seager presenting employees with twenty-five-year service awards at the Walsall Purse Co. in Glebe Street in the late 1970s. Left to right: Betty Cashmore, Mr Seager, Elsie ?, Ron Cornfield. John Bird (with beard in the second row) is now managing director of one of Walsall's largest remaining leathergoods companies, Daines & Hathaway.

Kath Steele preparing leathergoods at home for Nevada Leathergoods in 1998. Outworking or homeworking suits many women, particularly those with young children, and has a long history in Walsall. (Photograph courtesy of Chris Smart)

Kath Morrell bevelling an item at Peter Yates Leathergoods (formerly the factory of E. Hawley Ltd) in Hill Street in 1990. This firm specialised in fine-quality light leathergoods such as purses and wallets. Bevelling is the process of using a heated bevel to mark a 'tramline' around the edge of the item, which helps to consolidate the edge and visually makes the item look more 'finished'. (Photograph courtesy of Kate Green)

Joey Benfield at Whitehouse Cox in 1990, inspecting finished leathergoods. This is the final stage in the manufacture of leathergoods: any imperfections are noted and the work returned to the machinist or preparer for correction. Joey has recently celebrated forty-five years at Whitehouse Cox, and can be seen in the photograph on page 9. (Photograph courtesy of Kate Green)

A general view of the preparing shop at Peter Yates Leathergoods in 1990. Document cases are being made for Liberty of London. A gas pipe runs down the centre of the workshop, with individual jets providing heat for the bevels. Jars of stain (for finishing the cut edges of the leather) jostle with mugs of tea on the bench. (Photograph courtesy of Kate Green)

Walsall-made products are probably in every home in the country, yet despite this few of the town's manufacturers could truly be said to be household names. This chapter looks at three firms – Jabez Cliff, D. Mason & Sons, and Mark Cross – each of which became a leader in its own sphere.

Jabez Cliff

Royal Warrant Holder for saddlery and lorinery to HM The Queen, Jabez Cliff is one of the most celebrated names in the equestrian world. The company was founded in 1873 by Jabez Cliff, a bridlecutter by trade, in modest premises in Portland Street. In 1906 the firm acquired the long-established saddlers J.A. Barnsby, moving to Lower Forster Street and henceforth using the Barnsby name on all of their saddles. Despite declining demand for saddlery and harness after the First World War, the company continued to prosper by successfully diversifying into the making of sports goods, dog equipment, and soft luggage. The company also maintained a steady stream of army contract work, producing a huge range of items from kilt straps to drum horse saddles.

As riding for pleasure gained popularity in the 1960s Jabez Cliff was well placed to meet the growing demand for saddles and bridles, and today it has a flourishing international trade. Three of the founder's great great grandchildren are currently directors of the company, and they have recently been joined by James Hitchen, a member of the sixth generation.

Left: The first Jabez Cliff, founder of the company. Tragedy struck in 1881 when he and his two sons were killed by typhoid, within six months of each other. The business was rescued by his wife and daughter, and when the latter married Frederick Tibbits, a bridlecutter, he took over the running of the company.

Opposite below: Assembling building materials for the construction of J.A. Barnsby's Globe Works in Lower Forster Street, *c.*1901, acquired by Jabez Cliff in 1906. The Boer War was a very profitable time for most Walsall saddlers, resulting in a minor building boom. On the left of the photograph is the saddlery factory of Charles Greatrex & Sons. This building and the adjacent Globe Works are still the home of Jabez Cliff today.

Above: J.A. Barnsby was described in 1885 as having a 'larger number of [saddle] patterns than any other house in the trade…for the continental, South American, China, Japan, East and West Indian, Austalian and Canadian markets'. This photograph of the company's products dates from 1894.

A view of the firm's premises probably taken shortly after Jabez Cliff had acquired the neighbouring factory in 1926. Originally the home of Charles Greatrex & Sons, this building is one of Walsall's oldest surviving purpose-built saddlery factories, having been built around 1860.

The 1931 Wembley Cup Final, like those of the previous three years, used a Cliff's 'non-tear' Globe football. Cliff footballs were also used in the 1928 Olympic Games.

Above: A Globe football being hand sewn in around 1930. The balls are sewn inside out, and then turned the correct way round. Much of this work was done by women outworkers, working in their own homes.

Right: A company advertisement from the *Walsall Red Book*, 1925.

FOOTBALLS   **TENNIS BALLS**
Water Polo Balls   Rubber Cricket Balls
Punch Balls   Rubber Hockey Balls

Golf Bags
Travelling Goods
etc.

made throughout by

JABEZ CLIFF & CO. Ltd.,

GLOBE WORKS,

FORSTER STREET, WALSALL.

'Phone—331.

'Grams—"Cliff,
Walsall."

Codes—A B C 5th,
Marconi,
International.

Proprietors of
J. A. Barnsby & Sons,
Makers of
Fine Riding Saddlery.

Above: The Jabez Cliff display at the British Industries Fair in 1938 includes an impressive range of soft luggage and sports bags, as well as the company's own brand golf clubs, which were forged at the Lower Forster Street works.

Left: Sir Jabez Cliff Tibbits. The grandson of the founder, Sir Cliff joined the family firm in 1900. In his early years he travelled widely in Europe on behalf of the company, before eventually taking over the running of the business. A history of the company produced in 1973 noted 'he was to serve and guide the firm for a lifetime ... from the days when the horse was the major form of transport, through the lean years when riding was a luxury sport, to the present time when it has emerged as one of the most popular and expanding leisure activities'. Sir Cliff was knighted in 1948 for his public work in Walsall. He died in 1974, aged eighty-nine, having served the company for seventy-four years.

The aviation heroine Amy Johnson at Aldridge Airport, Walsall, in 1932, carrying a lightweight Cliff holdall, in canvas with leather trim. Zip-up luggage was first seen in Britain at the British Industries Fair in 1930 and despite some initial scepticism soon proved its worth.

Hand luggage from a Jabez Cliff catalogue of around 1935. Cliff's responded quickly to the opportunities offered by the new zip technology, introducing a range of lightweight bags which weighed less than half their solid leather equivalents. These were ideally suited to air travel.

Oliver Morton, seen here in the centre of the photograph, training apprentices Stafford Clark (left) and Nigel Smith (right) in saddle-making in 1948. Stafford Clark was the first apprentice to be indentured after the war, and is seen here 'setting the seat', the early stages of making a saddle. The tree has been fitted with webbing straps and saddle linen, and is now ready to be covered with serge and then stuffed with wool to provide a firm yet comfortable riding seat.

John Hammond and Lenny Law 'at the bench', making saddles at Jabez Cliff, sometime in the early 1970s to judge by the fashions!

Alf Chilton working on a pair of saddles for Prince Charles and Princess Anne. These were presented to the Queen on the occasion of her visit to Walsall in 1963, together with a matching pair of bridles. The company has had a long history of supplying the Royal Household, and was made a Royal Warrant Holder in 1990.

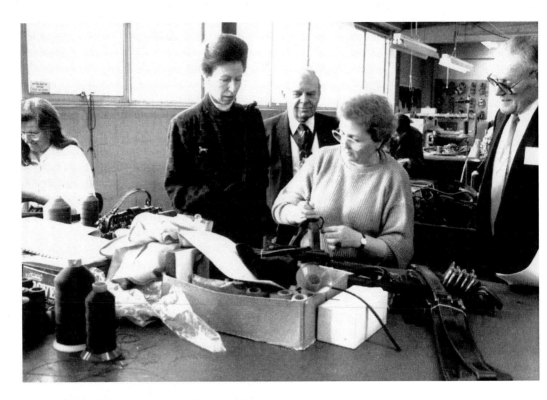

Above: A visit by the Princess Royal to Jabez Cliff in 1993. Leon Jessel, who is seen in the centre of the photograph, had recently succeeded the Princess Royal as Master of the Worshipful Company of Loriners. On the right of the photograph is Oliver Morton, who joined the company as an apprentice in 1929, eventually becoming chairman. Oliver is still working for the company after seventy-four years, at the age of eighty-eight.

Left: Arthur Groves constructing a saddle tree at Beebee & Beebee in 1998. This firm was taken over by Jabez Cliff in 1953 and relocated to an adjacent building. For centuries saddle trees were fashioned from solid wood, usually beech wood. Most saddle trees are now made from laminated birch plywood which is shaped in a press. (Photograph courtesy of Chris Smart)

D. Mason & Sons

Daniel Mason's is a classic nineteenth-century success story that could have come from the pages of a Victorian novel. Born in a remote part of Cardiganshire in 1808, as a young man he set out to make his fortune, walking all the way to Birmingham where he was first employed as a collarmaker. Through 'diligence and perseverance' he succeeded in working his way up to the position of foreman, before establishing his own company in 1853. Within a few years he was employing over a hundred people, and by the time of his death this figure had risen to 300, making it one of the largest saddlery and harness businesses in the country.

On Daniel Mason's death the company passed to his sons, who further expanded it and opened a Walsall factory in 1902. The company was proud to have supplied Captain Scott with dog harness in his Polar expedition of 1912. D. Mason & Sons continued to be managed as a family business until the 1960s.

Daniel Mason died a wealthy man in 1889, aged eighty-two: this photograph must have been taken near the end of his life.

A view of the company's premises in Bath Row, Birmingham, taken from the sale particulars of 1925, when the entire business relocated to Walsall. The site included three factories and thirteen houses, plus showrooms, a garage and an artesian well providing an 'inexhaustible supply of pure water'.

Daniel Mason's son Edward King Mason became a partner in the firm in 1872. He is seen here with his wife, Janet, and their children in the conservatory of their house in George Road, Edgbaston, Birmingham, c.1901. He and his brother Rowland further expanded the company after their father's death, opening a saddlery and harness factory in Walsall in 1902.

Saddlers at D. Mason & Sons, *c.*1910. Experienced male saddlers were the elite of the Walsall leather trade, earning up to 40s a week at a time when women stitchers were lucky to earn a quarter of that. Entry to the trade was controlled through a seven-year apprenticeship.

D. Mason & Sons acquired new premises in the heart of Walsall's leather quarter in Marsh Street, Walsall, in 1919, and, under various ownerships, traded from here for most of the twentieth century, making a wide range of leathergoods as well as saddlery and harness.

The company's stand at the British Leather Fair of 1931 shows how successfully the firm had adapted to meet the rising demand for small leathergoods, as the traditional market for saddlery and harness fell away.

The Marsh Street factory of D. Mason & Sons was conveniently situated a few yards from Walsall railway station, allowing for the rapid despatch of goods to customers. This is the 'home goods despatch' warehouse, c.1930. Tea chests are being carefully packed, ready for weighing on the scales to the right in the photograph.

The company's fleet of cars, used by their commercial travellers (or salesmen), seen here outside Maude's Garage in Wolverhampton Street in the 1920s.

The D. Mason & Sons 'social' at the Co-op Hall, 1931, was an annual event eagerly anticipated by the workforce. Daniel Mason's grandson Leonard K. Mason, the managing director of the company, is in the second row, third from the right. The company employed about 300 people at this date.

Above: Staff from D. Mason & Sons setting out on a works outing to Evesham in 1924, in a charabanc with solid tyres. Note the maximum speed – a stately 12mph!

Left: Daniel Mason's great grandson, Geoffrey Mason (centre), giving Sir Harry Goldsmid, MP for Walsall South, a tour of the Marsh Street factory in 1967. Geoffrey Mason was managing director of the company at this date. A squadron leader in the RAF during the Second World War, he had no children and was the last member of the Mason family to be involved in running the company.

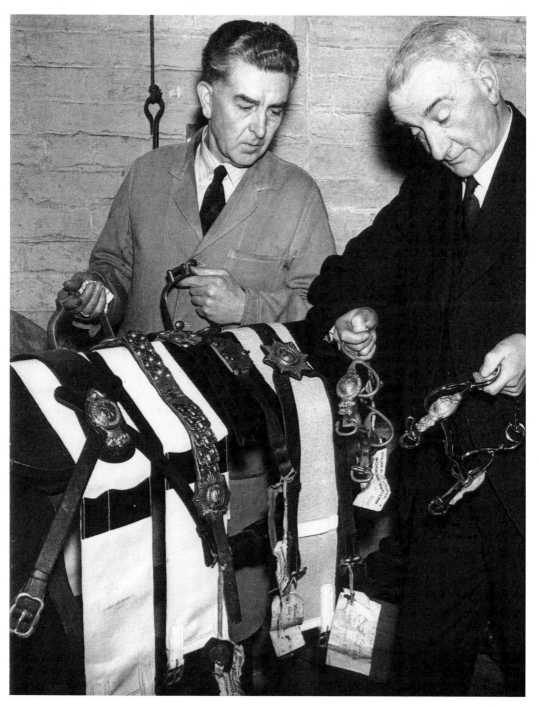

H. Jones and L.D. Stokes checking lorinery and harness for the Queen's coronation in 1953. D. Mason & Sons were regular suppliers of the saddlery and harness used in ceremonial duties by the Household Cavalry. Mr Stokes sadly noted how 'Demand for saddlery is greatly reduced … so it is pleasing to find one of Walsall's oldest industries will be represented in this ceremony'. (Photograph courtesy of *Walsall Observer*)

Mark Cross

Mark Cross is one of the most remarkable companies to have been associated with Walsall. Established in 1845 in Boston in the United States by an Irish saddler named Henry Cross, the company passed on his death to his son Mark. It was eventually acquired by an employee, Patrick Murphy. Under Murphy's ownership the firm relocated to New York and soon established a reputation as retailers of the very finest English saddlery and leathergoods, much of it Walsall made. Murphy had served part of his apprenticeship in Walsall, learning English saddlery skills, and eventually, around 1908, he bought out his English supplier. Thenceforth he operated his own factory in Warewell Street, Walsall, with shops in London, Paris and Milan as well as New York and Boston.

Patrick's remarkable son Gerald further developed Mark Cross. Gerald and his wife Sara had impeccable taste and brought an international sophistication to the company's products. They spent much of their time in France, alternating between Paris and the Villa America, their home in Cap d'Antibes. As wealthy members of the coterie of artists and intellectuals gathered in Paris in the 1920s they helped to finance the Diaghilev Ballet, and numbered F. Scott Fitzgerald, Cole Porter, and Ernest Hemingway among their closest friends. Picasso, another close friend, called Sara 'the divine Sara'. Fitzgerald's *Tender is the Night* is dedicated to Sara and Gerald, and the characters of Dick and Nicole Diver in that book are partly based on the couple.

The Murphys sold Mark Cross in 1948. The business continued to operate, but the Walsall factory was eventually acquired by D. Mason & Sons in 1961. It is still remembered locally for having employed many of the most skilled leatherworkers in the town, producing some of the finest quality leathergoods ever seen.

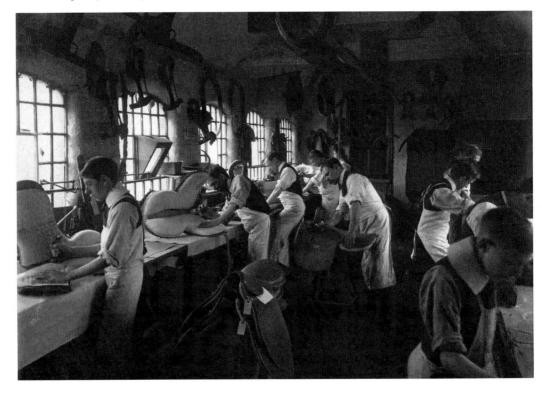

Above: A view of the case-making shop at Mark Cross, *c.*1910. A combination of hand sewing and machine sewing is taking place, with male preparers working by the windows. This and the following photographs were probably commissioned by the Murphys shortly after they had taken over the ownership of the Warewell Street factory from J. Harvey Page in around 1908.

Right: The suitcase-making workshop at Mark Cross, *c.*1910. Their catalogues of this period show that many of the cases had superb silver-plated fittings.

Opposite: Saddlery-making at Mark Cross, *c.*1910. English saddlery was much prized in the United States for its combination of strength, durability and elegant lines. A sidesaddle can be seen in the middle of the photograph. The young apprentice on the left is using a wooden masher to ensure that the wool flock stuffing of the saddle panel is evenly distributed.

Left: The ladies' bag department at Mark Cross, *c.*1910. Bundles of bag frames hang in the window. The gas pipes, which provided heat for the creasing tools (used to mark the edges of the leather with decorative 'tramlines'), can be seen running across the windows.

Below: Jewellery-box making at Mark Cross, *c.*1910. Cardboard shells or carcasses are being covered with leather to create strong yet light boxes. A well-used glue pot lies on the bench. Note that all of the work is being undertaken by hand. The small notice reads 'Smile – Damn You', an early example of workplace humour!

An indication of the quality of workmanship found at Mark Cross is that they produced their own locks and case fittings. Such attention to detail earned them an enviable reputation.

WORK BASKET
Table Model.

THE simplicity of this basket is its charm. The useful articles, well arranged in a strongly made basket of practical shape, will delight the enthusiastic needleworker.

Two sizes are made for increased convenience.

No. 1380. Finest Brown Wicker Basket, with Red, Green, Blue or Purple Long grained Leather or Natural Pigskin lids, linings in harmony.

No. 1379. Is similar, but the wicker is enamelled White, and the lids are of glazed Calfskin, pastel shades of Pink, Purple, Blue and Tan.

No. 1380.
10 × 8 × 3½ in., or 14 × 10 × 4 in.

WORK BASKET
Draw-top Model.

THE base is of very finely plaited willow and the draw-up top is watered silk in attractive shades. The circular pad which contains the sewing accessories fits into the bottom of the basket. This is a particularly dainty model and easily portable for work out of doors.

No. 3412. White Enamelled Wicker, with crushed leather pad and coloured silk tops. Pink, Helio, Blue.

No. 3412. Diameter of Basket, 7 in.

SEWING CASE
Roll up Model.

WHEN packing for a journey, articles which roll up are appreciated. This handy and compact little case contains a useful range of sewing accessories, and rolls most compactly, as will be seen from the dimensions given.

No. 2027. Art shades of Fine grained Leather. Green, Pink, Helio, Blue, or Tan Velvet Calfskin.

No. 2027. Size closed 6½ in.

A page from a Mark Cross catalogue, *c*.1920. The majority of the company's goods were produced in heavier bridle leathers and pigskin, which Gerald Murphy favoured as being distinctively English in character.

The Mark Cross fire team outside the Warewell Street factory during the Second World War.

A group of American servicemen standing outside the Mark Cross factory during Walsall's Anglo-American Friendship Week in February 1945. As part of the week's events, tours of local factories had been arranged, aimed at bringing about a greater understanding between the two nations. Note the 'V for victory' painted on the factory wall. (10299/AL)

Inside the Mark Cross factory, a group of GIs watching Mrs Tiny Hounslow making billfolds for the American market in 1945. The workbench paraphernalia of glue pot, marble, bottles of stain, and a gas burner are very typical of the industry at this date. (10303 /AL)

Taken from the same album as the previous photographs, this image is revealing in both the conditions in which luxury leathergoods were being made, and the age of the remaining Mark Cross workforce. All of the younger workers had presumably signed up for war service. (10302/ AL)

Above: Cutting out parts for a billfold by hand in 1945. As in the previous photographs, there is a marked absence of young workers.

Right: A page from a Mark Cross catalogue of 1958. The company was still making superb quality goods for the luxury market, and in 1954 its luggage had featured in Alfred Hitchcock's film *Rear Window.*

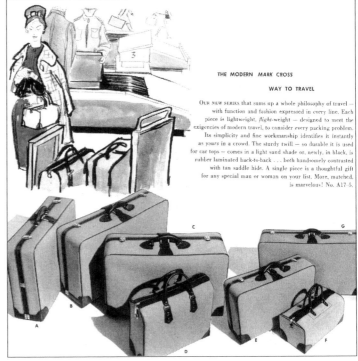

THE MODERN MARK CROSS

WAY TO TRAVEL

OUR NEW SERIES that sums up a whole philosophy of travel — with function and fashion expressed in every line. Each piece is lightweight, *flight*-weight — designed to meet the exigencies of modern travel, to consider every packing problem. Its simplicity and fine workmanship identifies it instantly as *yours* in a crowd. The sturdy twill — so durable it is used for car tops — comes in a light sand shade or, newly, in black, is rubber laminated back-to-back . . . both handsomely contrasted with tan saddle hide. A single piece is a thoughtful gift for any special man or woman on your list. More, matched, is marvelous! No. A17-5.

five

Glove-making

Probably the least well known of Walsall's major leather trades, glove-making flourished for a period of about fifty years after 1920. The introduction of the trade seems to have been a direct response to the decline of the town's traditional saddlery and harness trade, which made diversification a necessity. The first gloving companies were established after the First World War and the number steadily increased so that by 1940 there were six in operation. By the latter date a wide variety of gloves was being made, ranging from heavy leather hedging mitts to delicate gloves in the finest doeskin, for formal evening wear. The manufacture of the lighter types of gloves called for a high degree of skill, and it was said that eighty-six separate operations were needed to make a single pair of gloves. Some of the key personnel, such as the all-important cutters, were recruited from established centres of the trade, such as Worcester and the Somerset town of Yeovil.

The trade was still booming in the 1960s, producing gloves for a range of niche markets such as golfing and motoring, as well as the general fashion market, but within a few years it had been largely destroyed by the impact of cheap imports from South Korea and Japan. Walsall's last glove-making company, Kingsman, produced a wide range of items including gloves for cycling and yachting, and motorbike gauntlets for the police but it too eventually closed in 1998.

'Making Gloves for Motoring, Agricultural and Works Use' at D. Mason & Sons in Marsh Street, *c.*1930.

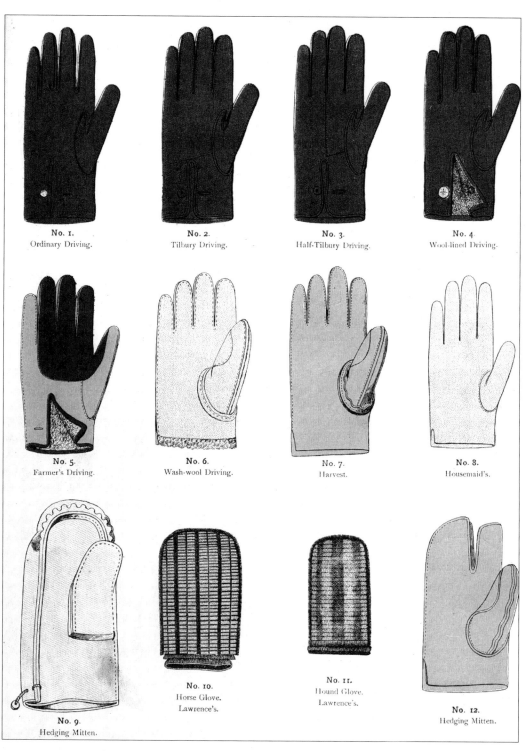

No. 1.
Ordinary Driving.

No. 2.
Tilbury Driving.

No. 3.
Half-Tilbury Driving.

No. 4
Wool-lined Driving.

No. 5.
Farmer's Driving.

No. 6.
Wash-wool Driving.

No. 7.
Harvest.

No. 8.
Housemaid's.

No. 9.
Hedging Mitten.

No. 10.
Horse Glove.
Lawrence's.

No. 11.
Hound Glove.
Lawrence's.

No. 12.
Hedging Mitten.

Heavy-duty gloves and mittens for agricultural and industrial use were being made as a sideline by D. Mason & Sons by 1900. Such products were designed to be functional rather than stylish.

Mr Howard Power of the firm of D. Power & Sons in 1922. Originally established in 1846, up until the time of the First World War the company was primarily a manufacturer of horse clothing, saddlery and small leathergoods. After the war they began manufacturing gloves. The new business proved so successful that within a few years they had increased their team of cutters from two to twenty.

Left: Mrs Fortescue, wife of one of the D. Power & Sons salesmen, models a pair of hand-stitched leather gauntlets, *c*.1924. Power & Sons seem to have pioneered the manufacture of ladies gloves in Walsall.

Opposite below: Hand cutting at G.H.T. Madeley in Station Street, *c*.1935. The stretched leather is being cut into various glove components such as 'tranks', 'thumbs' and 'fourchettes'. Patterns for tranks can be seen hanging on the wall and on the bench on the left. Among those present is Bob Tuck, furthest from the camera, who came from Yeovil.

Left: Cutters were the aristocrats of the gloving trade, just as they were in the light leathergoods trade. It was said that it was here that the company's profits were either made or lost. There was great skill in stretching the leather correctly to ensure that it would retain its shape once in daily use, and in cutting each skin to obtain the greatest number of glove components, making allowance for holes and marks in the leather. A good cutter would take up to five years to train. Here Les Hawes is stretching a skin over the edge of a bench at Stuart Madeley in Marsh Street. One hand keeps the skin securely anchored while the other stretches it.

The press shop at G.H.T. Madeley, *c*.1935. On the central bench bundles of glove components are waiting to be 'numerated' with stamps. This was apprentices' work and was done to ensure that all of the components for each pair of gloves could be reunited after press cutting. It was vital that all of the components matched exactly. Webbing presses can be seen on the left and right of the photograph.

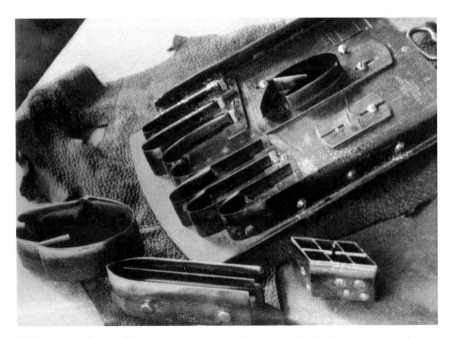

'Webbs' or pattern knives. The various parts of the glove have already been cut out, and are now shaped more precisely using a webb. The leather is placed on the gutta percha bed of the press, the webb placed face down on the leather, and a lever is pulled to slide the whole assemblage under the press.

The machining shop at G.H.T. Madeley, c.1935. The glove components, having been precisely trimmed to size in the webbing press, are now being machine sewn together. This was also skilled work and it was considered that it took three years before a machinist was fully competent.

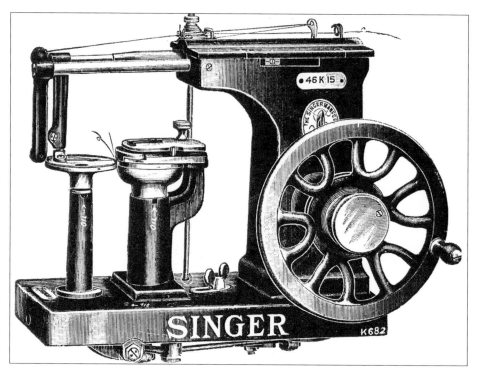

A prixseam sewing machine. In prixseam sewing, the pieces of leather are brought together back to back with the edges exposed, and then stitched parallel to the edge. The needle usually operates on a horizontal plane.

Above: Hand stitching gloves at G.H.T. Madeley, *c.*1935. Hand sewing was slower than machine sewing, but the finished gloves could command a higher price. In some areas a stitching 'donkey' or clamp was used to hold the gloves while being stitched, but in Walsall the gloves appear to have normally been sewn freehand. The women on the right of the picture are 'ironing' the finished gloves, by placing them over a heated 'hand' to remove any creases or wrinkles.

Left: Glovecutters on the fire escape at the former G.H.T. Madeley works in Station Street in 1938. By this date the company had been taken over by Whitehouse Cox, and was trading as Stuart Madeley. From top to bottom: Mr Williams, Harry Marshall, Bill Simpson, Bill Giles, Jack Ceney and Horace Lloyd.

Above: Staking gloving leather to make it more supple at the Yeovil tanners C.W. Pittard. There were close links between Walsall and Yeovil, with a number of the Walsall gloving firms purchasing their leather from Yeovil tanneries. Some Walsall glovers also sub-contracted glove orders to Yeovil companies when they had more work than they could cope with.

Right: Derek Wright cutting leather at Stuart Madeley in 1953. The cutter's shears are clearly visible, and the cardboard trank patterns can be seen on the wall behind.

Left: An unnamed glover measuring leather with a size stick. These tapered sticks were usually marked in inches. Glove sizing is based on the measurement around the width of the hand.

Below: The gloving shop at Stuart Madeley in Marsh Street, *c.*1965. Such workshops could be very friendly places to work in, despite the often long hours and spells of intense pressure to complete an order.

Above: Edna Kirby of Tarantella, *c.*1970. Having trained at D. Powers in Long Street, Edna saved up enough money to buy her own sewing machine and began making gloves from home. Her business was a great success. She eventually became a major supplier to Marks & Spencer and was particularly successful in the American market. Driving and golfing gloves were a speciality of the firm. (Photograph courtesy of *Birmingham Post*)

Right: A machinist at Tarantella, *c.*1970, stitching a badge onto the back of a golfing glove. Edna Kirby employed many young women workers and opened a pioneering crèche to care for their pre-school age children, something that was still very unusual at the time. (Photograph courtesy of *Birmingham Post*)

Bill Lloyd, foreman cutter at Tarantella, *c*.1970. The Tarantella factory was sited in a former tannery, at the junction of Hatherton Street and Littleton Street. (Photograph courtesy of *Birmingham Post*)

Ironing a glove at Tarantella, c.1970. The glove has been placed over a metal hand that has been heated by a thermostat-controlled electric element. The creases are being gently removed using a bone folder. (Photograph courtesy of *Birmingham Post*)

Doreen Stokes being presented with a long service award at the Leather Museum after thirty-seven years in the gloving trade by David Anderson, Master of the Worshipful Company of Glovers. Doreen worked for Kingsman, the last of Walsall's gloving companies, which closed in 1998.

An impressive array of Tarantella products, c.1970. The firm also had a flourishing line in making suede skirts at this date! (Photograph courtesy of *Birmingham Post*)

six

Specialist
Trades

It was the proud boast of Walsall's late nineteenth-century saddlers that they could supply 'everything for the horse'. Alongside the saddlery and harness trades were a number of related specialist trades, which helped to ensure that this was not an idle claim. The presence of whipmakers, brushmakers, curry-comb makers, saddle-tree makers, makers of May Day decorations and horse brasses, bits, stirrups and spurs, horse clothing, saddler's tools and stable fittings, to name just a selection, meant that by 1900 Walsall probably had Europe's greatest concentration of equestrian suppliers.

On the back of this concentration of specialist skills a host of new trades developed or expanded after 1900. Falling outside the normal definition of light leathergoods, these trades included makers of sports equipment, dog accessories, clothing and heavy luggage. Most Walsall companies specialised in just one trade, although some of the biggest such as Jabez Cliff and D. Mason & Sons covered a wider range, making them more resilient to fluctuations in demand.

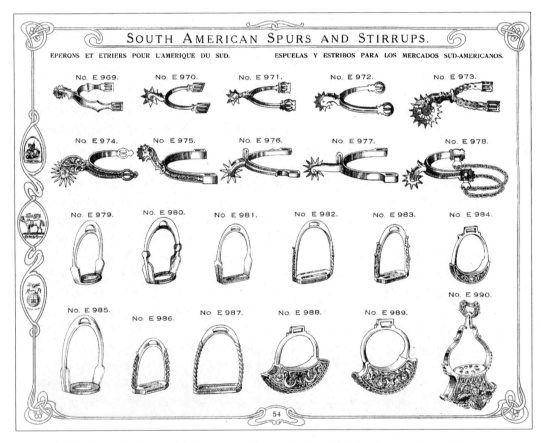

The Walsall leather trade has its origins in the town's medieval trade in bits stirrups and spurs, known as 'lorinery'. In the nineteenth century South America became a major market for Walsall's loriners, and local firms produced a wide range of special products for this market including lasso rings and bombillas – tubes for drinking the gaucho's favourite maté drink.

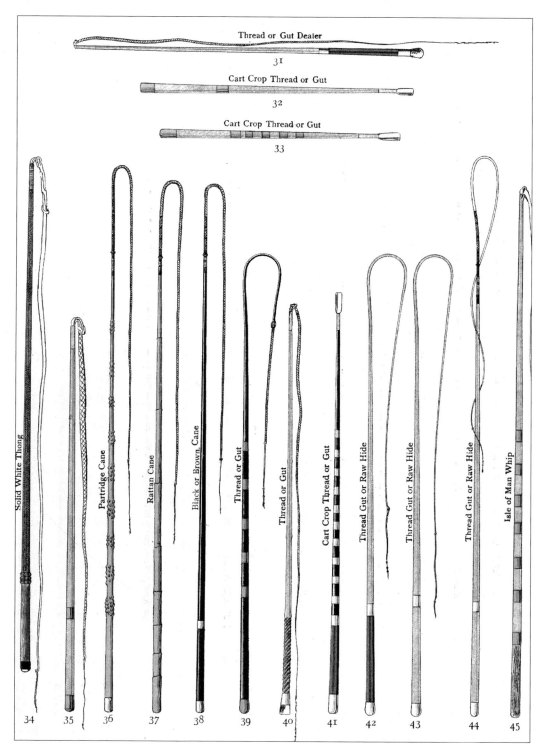

Thread or Gut Dealer

31

Cart Crop Thread or Gut

32

Cart Crop Thread or Gut

33

Solid White Thong

Partridge Cane

Rattan Cane

Black or Brown Cane

Thread or Gut

Thread or Gut

Cart Crop Thread or Gut

Thread Gut or Raw Hide

Thread Gut or Raw Hide

Thread Gut or Raw Hide

Isle of Man Whip

34   35   36   37   38   39   40   41   42   43   44   45

Whip-making was one of the first leather trades to become established in Walsall in the early nineteenth century. Four whip and whip-thong makers were recorded in the census of 1801.

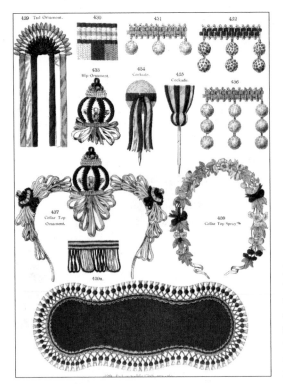

May Day parades of horse-drawn vehicles were a feature in the life of many Victorian communities, and the making of May Day decorations represented another of Walsall's specialist cottage industries. The decorations usually included elaborate harness trimmings made from silk ribbon, wool, and man-made materials.

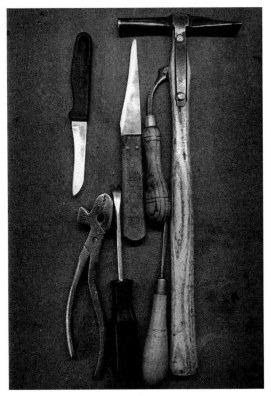

The production of saddler's tools was another important specialist trade which became established in the town in the early nineteenth century, and which survives to this day. This assortment of tools from a Walsall saddler's bench includes a tacking hammer and a pair of pincers or pliers used in the straining of webbing and leather for the saddle seat. (Photograph courtesy of Chris Smart)

Above: The beltmaking workshop at D. Mason & Sons in Marsh Street, *c.*1930. This company, and its subsidiary John Leckie & Co, were official suppliers of Boy Scouts and Girl Guides belts.

Right: Tracey Fulford plaiting a fashion belt at Whitehouse Cox Ltd in Marsh Street, Walsall, in 1990. These belts were produced by Whitehouse Cox for the American company Ralph Lauren Ltd. (Photograph courtesy of Kate Green)

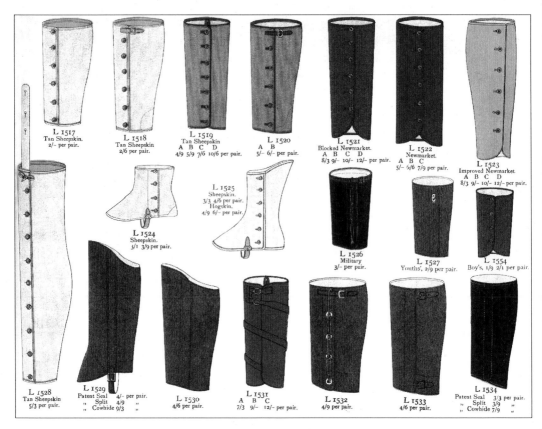

L 1517
Tan Sheepskin,
2/- per pair.

L 1518
Tan Sheepskin
2/6 per pair.

L 1519
Tan Sheepskin
A   B   C   D
4/9 5/9 7/6 10/6 per pair.

L 1520
A   B
5/- 6/- per pair.

L 1521
Blocked Newmarket.
A   B   C   D
8/3 9/- 10/- 12/- per pair.

L 1522
Newmarket.
A   B   C
5/- 6/6 7/9 per pair.

L 1523
Improved Newmarket
A   B   C   D
8/3 9/- 10/- 12/- per pair.

L 1525
Sheepskin.
3/3 4/6 per pair.
Hogskin.
4/9 6/- per pair.

L 1524
Sheepskin.
3/1 3/9 per pair.

L 1526
Military
3/- per pair.

L 1527
Youths', 2/9 per pair.

L 1554
Boy's, 1/9 2/1 per pair.

L 1528
Tan Sheepskin
5/3 per pair.

L 1529
Patent Seal   4/- per pair.
  „   Split   4/9   „
  „   Cowhide 9/3   „

L 1530
4/6 per pair.

L 1531
A   B   C
7/3 9/- 12/- per pair.

L 1532
4/9 per pair.

L 1533
4/6 per pair.

L 1534
Patent Seal   3/3 per pair.
  „   Split   3/9   „
  „   Cowhide 7/9   „

Above: Leggings and Gaiters' from a John Leckie & Co. catalogue of the 1890s. A Walsall directory of 1916 noted 'for those who have to move about in wet weather, for horseback riding, sporting, or field work of any description, leggings are an almost indispensible part of their equipment ... in tropical countries they protect the wearer against bites of snakes...'

Opposite above: 'Bags and Cases' from a John Leckie & Co. catalogue dating from the 1890s. Victorian luggage was built to last. These examples would have been made from solid cowhide stretched over sturdy metal frames, with solid brass fittings, and were probably entirely hand stitched. Note that the Gladstone bag (bottom centre) does not resemble the modern idea of such a bag!

Opposite below: The case-making workshop at D. Mason & Sons in Marsh Street, *c.*1930.

These Prices only represent some of our Best Selling Lines, but we make cheaper qualities, and also more expensive Goods.

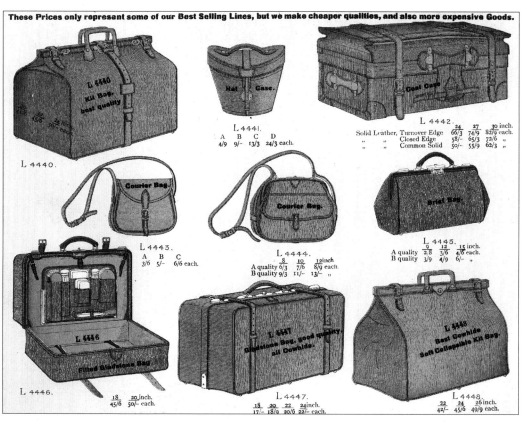

L 4440.
KH Bag, best quality.

L 4440.

Hat Case.

L 4441.

A	B	C	D
4/9	9/-	13/3	24/3 each.

Coat Case.

L 4442.

	24	27	30 inch.
Solid Leather, Turnover Edge	66/3	74/9	82/9 each.
,, ,, Closed Edge	58/-	65/3	72/6 ,,
,, ,, Common Solid	50/-	55/9	62/3 ,,

Courier Bag.

Courier Bag.

Brief Bag.

L 4443.

A	B	C
3/6	5/-	6/6 each.

L 4444.

	8	10	12 inch.
A quality	6/3	7/6	8/9 each.
B quality	9/3	11/-	13/- ,,

L 4445.

	9	12	15 inch.
A quality	2/8	3/6	4/6 each.
B quality	3/9	4/9	6/- ,,

L 4446

Fitted Gladstone Bag

L 4446.

18	20 inch.
45/6	50/- each.

L 4447.
Gladstone Bag, good quality, all Cowhide.

L 4447.

18	20	22	24 inch.
17/-	18/9	20/6	22/- each.

L 4448.
Best Cowhide
Soft Collapsible KH Bag.

L 4448.

22	24	26 inch.
42/-	45/6	49/9 each.

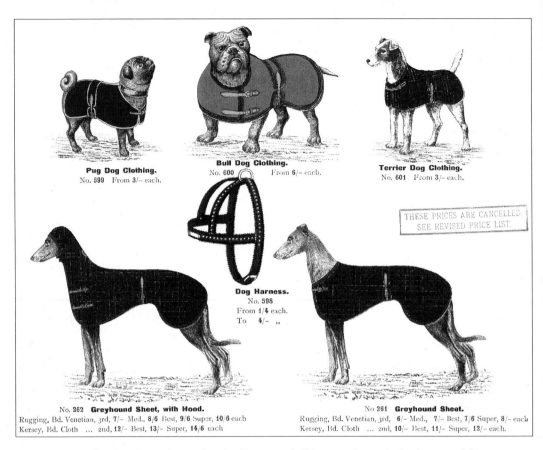

Pug Dog Clothing.
No. 599 From **3**/- each.

Bull Dog Clothing.
No. 600 From **6**/- each.

Terrier Dog Clothing.
No. 601 From **3**/- each.

THESE PRICES ARE CANCELLED.
SEE REVISED PRICE LIST.

Dog Harness.
No. 598
From **1/4** each.
To **4**/- „

No. 262 **Greyhound Sheet, with Hood.**
Rugging, Bd. Venetian, 3rd, **7**/- Med., **8/6** Best, **9/6** Super, **10/6** each
Kersey, Bd. Cloth ... 2nd, **12**/- Best, **13**/- Super, **14/6** each

No 261 **Greyhound Sheet.**
Rugging, Bd. Venetian, 3rd, **6**/- Med., **7**/- Best, **7/6** Super, **8**/- each
Kersey, Bd. Cloth ... 2nd, **10**/- Best, **11**/- Super, **12**/- each.

Dog equipment from a John Leckie catalogue of 1906. Walsall became the UK's chief centre of this trade in the early twentieth century, and fifteen local makers of dog collars were listed in 1940. A number of local metalworking firms such as Eylands produced the buckles, swivels and rings needed for such equipment.

Eileen Mason punching holes in dog collars at Whitehouse Cox in Marsh Street in 1990. A lead weight keeps the collars in place; the spacing of the holes would normally be done by eye. A bundle of hole punches of different gauges lies on the bench. (Photograph courtesy of Kate Green)

Leather clothing was not a major element in the town's 'hundred trades', but during the 1920s and 1930s a number of local firms experimented with this market. Patterson & Stone, originally founded as a harness maker, was clearly a resourceful firm, since the model sports one of the company's 'Crichton' shooting sticks with a leather seat, as well as a leather coat.

Above: Cutters at H. Bednall in 1939. Harry Bednall established Walsall's best-known leather clothing manufacturers after the First World War. Having trained as saddler he saw the opportunities presented by the increasing popularity of motorcars and motorbikes, and produced a range of protective leather clothing including jackets, waistcoats, gaiters, caps, and his own patented design of helmet.

Above: An impressive Patterson & Stone stand at the British Industries Fair in 1934. The products on display include the 'Eezwate' golf bag and the 'Expando' belt, plus a variety of leather and suede jackets.

Opposite below: During the Second World War Bednall's factory in Eldon Street was 'crammed with workers' making flying helmets and fur-lined jackets for the RAF. The business was sold to Adastra in 1957. These ski caps are from an H. Bednall catalogue of 1960.

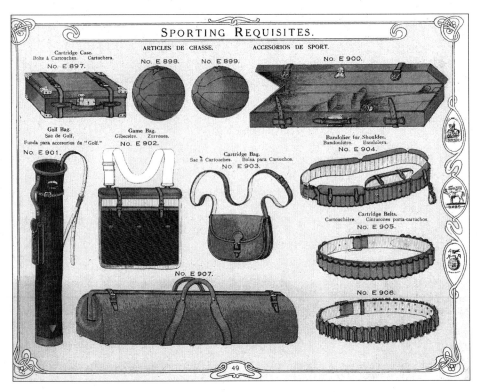

A selection of sporting equipment from a D. Mason & Sons catalogue, c.1905. The manufacture of sports balls was an important specialised sideline for several local manufacturers between the two world wars. The multilingual captions reflect the importance of Walsall's export trade.

Among the more bizarre products of the Walsall leather trades: giant medicine balls used as fairground pushballs. These Jabez Cliff staff, photographed c.1932, are, from left to right: Arthur Gradwell, Edie Pritchard, Maud Reynolds and George Babb.

seven

Walsall Leather Museum

Most of the photographs in this book have been drawn from the collections of the Walsall Leather Museum. The museum was opened fifteen years ago by Walsall MBC in response to local demand that more should be done to celebrate Walsall's unique place in the history of leatherworking. Consultation with the community showed that people wanted to see live demonstrations of leathercrafts as well as displays of historic and contemporary locally made leathergoods and saddlery, and somewhere to buy Walsall-made products.

The museum opened in 1988 and shortly afterwards won the Best Museum of Social or Industrial History award in the Museum of the Year Awards. Since 1988 the museum has built up major collections of artefacts, photographs, books, trade catalogues and sound recordings relating to the leather trade. The museum has a thriving programme of events as well as regular exhibitions, a flourishing shop selling Walsall-made leathergoods, and a popular café and meeting room, all of which have combined to give it an important place in the local community.

The buildings now occupied by the Leather Museum were originally constructed in 1891 by J. Withers & Son for the production of lorinery, or saddlers' ironmongery. They must once have towered over the surrounding streets of terraced houses.

Above: The Littleton Street limestone mines, *c.*1900. The neighbourhood of the Leather Museum was extensively mined for limestone in the nineteenth century. The limestone was mostly used as a flux in the smelting of iron ore, although some was burnt in limekilns located on the site of the museum. By the end of the century most of the mines were worked out, leaving a legacy of collapsing ground, which blighted large areas of the town until the 1980s.

Right: Gainsborough Handbag employees, *c.*1949, standing in what are now the museum gardens. The company was one of the main suppliers of handbags to Marks & Spencer, mostly made in synthetic materials. Working conditions in the factory are remembered as somewhat primitive, with staircases 'like ladders'. The chimney of the Wisemore Foundry of Malleable Ltd can be seen in the background.

By the mid-1980s the buildings were in poor condition, with the legacy of over ninety years of industrial usage all too apparent. They had become a highly visible eyesore on the town's main ringroad.

In 1987-1988 Walsall MBC completely refurbished the site, using funding from the European Regional Development Fund. The limestone mines were infilled, and the buildings were stabilised and comprehensively refurbished. Care was taken to preserve as much of their original character as possible. The planting in the gardens was chosen to tell the story of how trees and shrubs have been used in the tanning of leather.

The official opening of the Leather Museum by HRH the Princess Royal on 10 June 1988. The museum was developed as a living and working site, giving visitors the opportunity to meet leatherworkers and to see craft skills practised. Here expert bridlecutter Frank Egan discusses his trade with the Princess in the museum's bridlecutting workshops. (Photograph courtesy of *Birmingham Post*)

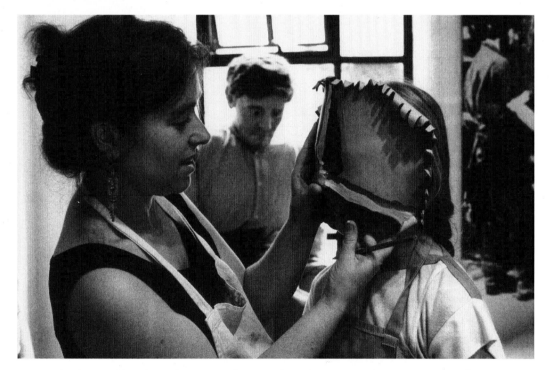

Over the past fifteen years the museum has earned a wide reputation for its programme of events and activities. During this time most of the leading leatherworkers in the country have held workshops at the museum, which have given people of all ages opportunities to learn new skills and find outlets for their creativity. Val Michael, who is seen in this photograph, has an international reputation as both a leatherworker and an inspirational tutor.

Right: The author and his colleague Francesca Cox celebrate the museum's tenth anniversary in 1998. In its first ten years the museum received nearly 300,000 visitors from all parts of the world. (Picture courtesy of *Wolverhampton Express and Star*)

Below: Jack Halksworth was a much-loved member of the demonstrator team at the museum from its inception. With the exception of a spell of service as a wireless telegrapher in India, Italy and Malaya during the Second World War, Jack spent a lifetime in the leathergoods industry, of which he had an unrivalled knowledge. He was a foreman at John More & Co., supervising the handbag department, and for many years worked as a lecturer at the Leathergoods Training Centre, part of Walsall College of Art. As a demonstrator at the Leather Museum he relished the opportunity to share his love for the subject with visitors of all ages. After a period of ill health, Jack died in May 2001.

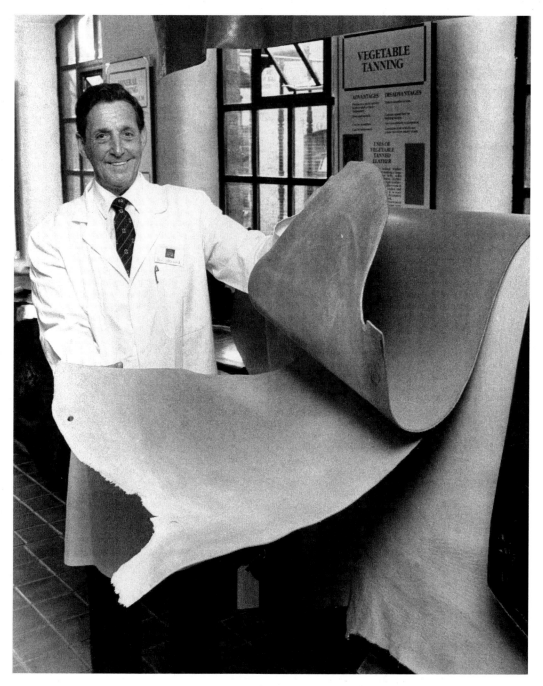

Museum currying demonstrator Ron Hawkins. Ron comes from a family with a long history of leatherworking, and for many years worked at the Park Street tannery of E.T. Holden, before that firm relocated to Scotland in 1970. Ron then moved to work for the curriers J. & E. Sedgwick. Since retirement he has become a valued member of the Leather Museum's team. Ron's enthusiasm for his subject is legendary!